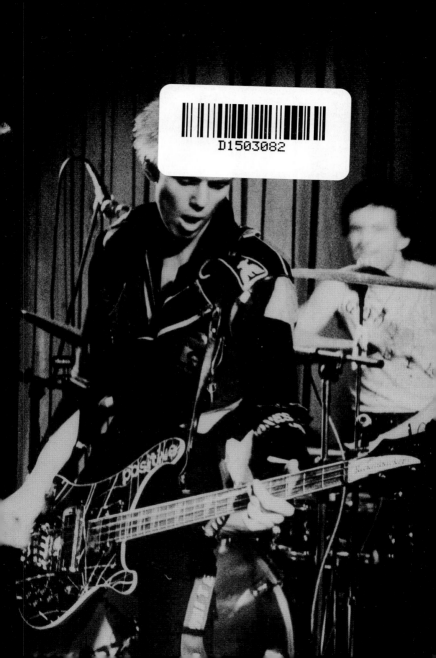

MODERN ICONS

THE CLASH

Acknowledgments

With very grateful thanks to Philip Dodd, Lucinda Hawksley,
Helen Johnson, Morse Modaberi and to John Stickland,
Gary Stickland and the staff of the National
Sound Archive for their help in the research of this book.

Paul Du Noyer started his career on *NME*, before joining the launch team of *Q*
magazine. He was editor of *Q* between 1990 and 1992, and then became the
founding editor of the hugely influential monthly magazine *Mojo*, picking up an Editor
of the Year award in 1994. He left *Mojo* in 1995, but remains a contributing editor.
In 1997 he wrote *We all shine on*, a book about the solo songs of John Lennon.

Modern Icons conceived and developed
for and with Virgin Publishing Ltd by Flame Tree Publishing,
a part of The Foundry Creative Media Company Limited,
The Long House, Antrobus Road, Chiswick, London W4 5HY.

ISBN 0-312-17939-1

Library of Congress Cataloging-in-Publication Data available on request

First published in the United Kingdom in 1997 by Virgin Publishing Ltd.

First U.S. edition

10 9 8 7 6 5 4 3 2 1

MODERN ICONS

THE CLASH

Introduction by Paul Du Noyer

St. Martin's Press

New York

CONTENTS

INTRODUCTION

R ight from the start you knew The Clash were a great punk rock band. But they became more than that. All these years later they stand as one of the greatest rock bands of all time. The Rolling Stones, The Who, Led Zeppelin – those same 'dinosaur' acts that The Clash began by metaphorically gobbing on – are now the very bands in whose illustrious company they are ranked. The Clash's career was not so very long, but they played with a passionate intensity that will never be forgotten by anyone who saw them. For a group with no pretensions to musical virtuosity, they forged a sound that still surges with the power, grandeur and range that distinguishes the best rock'n'roll from all the rest. In their time they were accused of every crime conceivable, from folly and hypocrisy to outright betrayal. And none of it has dented their legend one little bit. The Clash have gone down in history as something besides another rock career. They are a kind of heroic myth. Their story is an epic adventure.

The Clash endure as icons, not purely because of their music – which, as even their diehard fans admit, was not consistently brilliant, and rarely matched the sulphurous excitement of their stage act. They're also remembered for their flawed idealism, as a band who stood for something above and beyond commercial success. Rebellion has been part of the rock'n'roll package ever since the young Elvis Presley first curled his lip into a sneer and swivelled his hips to the consternation of adult America. The Clash's brand of rebel rock was different. It had a political edge – rebels with a cause – that didn't mean much to their later audience in the States, but made them ringleaders of the British punk revolution. They were not philosophers, and many have questioned the sincerity and coherence of the band's ideology, but for a few glorious years they walked it like they talked it and they were an inspiration to thousands.

Even more importantly, perhaps, The Clash just looked right. Rock'n'roll is a visual phenomenon as much as it is anything else, and The Clash invented an image for themselves that burned its way into a million memories. The British punk groups were not a glamorous

bunch, and mostly took an obstinate pride in looking as defiantly wrong as they could manage. But The Clash arrived with a style as sharp and well-considered as the English mods of a decade before. As they grew in confidence and stature, so they developed an outlaw swagger that confirmed them as the most photogenic act of the era, every inch 'the Last Gang in Town' of one of their typically romantic, vainglorious song titles. Once again, the authenticity of the band's guerilla chic is a topic that can be endlessly debated: to this day there are some who scorn them as the pop stars who once flew into war-torn Belfast simply for a photo session. Still, as sheer spectacle, The Clash's stance injected yet another dimension of drama into their art.

Finally, of course, there was their name. The Clash. It was perfect for the moment when they formed, perfect for the music that they made, and has gone on to serve their legend just as well. The group was born in a time of cultural conflict and they never found themselves at ease for as long as they lasted. They lived and worked amid the din of colliding opposites, and could not resolve the contradictions at their heart. True to their name, The Clash never did achieve stability or permanence, and the tensions they embodied would eventually pull them apart.

The group's eventual members had grown up in an age when rock music was not merely a consumer pastime, but a matter of fierce personal allegiance. Like many other teenagers of the early Seventies, they came to share a disillusioned sense that rock's sheer success had removed it from the generation it used to represent. The pomp and splendour of globally-feted acts such as Queen, Elton John and ELO no longer spoke to the hearts and minds of

young firebrands who wanted music to express their lives, fears, hopes, energy and frustrations. Young Londoners such as Joe Strummer, Mick Jones and Paul Simonon started looking elsewhere – to reggae, with its righteous zeal and apocalyptic rhetoric; and to pub rock, the raw, stripped-down minimalism of hard-driving local acts like Dr Feelgood.

There was a discontent, too, about Britain in 1976, where the economic optimism and cultural vitality of the Sixties had given way to stagnation. The street politics of right and left drew on a reservoir of pessimism among the young. This strangely demoralised climate, when combined with musical stalemate, threw up the first

wave of London punks, led by The Sex Pistols. Already attempting to start a band with Bernie Rhodes, an associate of the Pistols's manager Malcolm McLaren, the aforementioned Jones and Simonon recruited Joe Strummer from a struggling pub rock act, The 101'ers, attracted by the hoarse desperation of his singing. The musicians' very lack of ability – Strummer had changed his name from Mellor to emphasise his rudimentary skills, while Simonon had never picked up an instrument in his life – only helped to fire their intensity. Extremism of attitude was a punk virtue, and The Clash shared an almost puritanical vision of rock, as a channel for their angry impatience with society and pop music alike. Simonon, as the most aesthetically-aware member, perfected the group's sensational dress, chiefly the paint-splattered fatigues, the noose-like ties and thuggish boots, and the McLaren-inspired use of provocative stencilled slogans reading 'Hate & War', 'Sten Guns In Knightsbridge' and 'Creative Violence'.

Now managed by Rhodes, they signed to the giant corporation CBS – an act of collusion with the capitalist enemy that haunted them to the end – and with the drummer Terry Chimes made their first album. Self-titled, this record remains a definitive punk artefact. It appeared in April 1977, a full six months before the Sex Pistols's first LP, and every track still stands as an insurrectionary anthem of its time: 'Career Opportunities', 'White Riot', 'London's Burning' and the

rest. While Strummer's urgent howls were all but indecipherable, the hyperactive ranting, the explosive, amphetamine momentum of the sound and confrontational style of the packaging were all unmistakable calls to the cultural barricade. Other early songs set out the group's manifesto more plainly: in '1977' Strummer declared 'No Beatles, Elvis or Rolling Stones', while 'White Man In Hammersmith Palais' derided entertainers who were using the banner of rebellion to make money. In the Queen's Jubilee Year of 1977, attitudes in Britain were polarised as never before, with The Clash installed as spokesmen for the radical side of a national divide.

Defiantly one-dimensional, the group's sound was, at first, as savage a brute as anyone had ever encountered. Even the Pistols and The Damned had an orthodox melodic pulse beneath their bluster, but The Clash's style was pure sonic assault. Relentlessly fast, militantly frill-free, it was a cauldron of crude riffing and

hoarse imploring. When the world's bedroom insurrectionaries and garage thrashers were first inspired to form their own punk bands, they used The Clash as their blueprint: it wasn't just the fiercest noise around, it seemed like the easiest to imitate.

Yet Strummer's rasp and Jones's angry guitar were possessed of a greater emotional punch than most of their admirers could muster.

Over the years to follow, they would increase their dynamic range and display an unsuspected degree of stylistic ambition – especially under the spacious influence of dub reggae – that kept them interesting to the end, even when their reach exceeded their grasp. All the way from '48 Hours' to 'Straight To Hell', Strummer and Jones were songwriters of underrated scope.

They acquired a new drummer in Topper Headon, toured with The Sex Pistols and – once Johnny Rotten's band had disintegrated – became the boss punk rock act. They defined the movement's style, with imagery of dole queues and towerblocks (although their own proletarian links were tenuous), social oppression and militant resistance to the rising tide of right wing racialism. Despite this oppositional stance, the force and expanding range of their music saw The Clash gaining mainstream popularity. By the time of their second and third albums – 'Give 'Em Enough Rope' and 'London Calling', respectively – the band was gaining ground in America, with global acceptance not far behind. Already they felt the sting of a backlash from their earliest supporters, including the UK music press whose regular interviews were The Clash's chief means of spreading their message. A band supposedly

at one with their audience, identified with all who were excluded from the system, would always find success a tough concept to handle. In fact The Clash were in perpetual dispute with their employers at CBS, who were hardly won over by the release of a sprawling, unfocused triple-album called 'Sandinista!'. And they made a virtue of boycotting Britain's weekly TV showcase, *Top Of The Pops*. But to the cynics, and to the hardliners who had once lionised the band for its principles, The Clash were either shallow phonies or class traitors.

Throughout their career the band retained a certain delinquent credibility. There was a gratifying stream of news stories: Clash members were routinely being arrested, fined or briefly imprisoned for offences including drunkenness, pilfering from hotels, or even shooting at pigeons. After one such brush with the law they renamed a series of gigs the 'Out on Parole' tour. Meant to be tongue-in-cheek, the gesture only fuelled accusations of trite rebel posturing.

Just as the undisciplined mess of 'Sandinista!' suggested a band in some internal disarray, so The Clash's international stature made the early Eighties a tortured time for them. In 1982 they were to be seen at New York's Shea Stadium, supporting The Who on one of their so-called 'farewell' tours. The US

audience took to Strummer and co. enthusiastically, acclaiming them as a powerful, orthodox rock band much in the tradition of the headline act. But, like so many of their old UK fans, the band was uncomfortably aware of how closely they now resembled the establishment entertainers they once despised. Their next album, 'Combat Rock', was maybe the slickest thing they had ever produced, and

certainly carried a few of their finest moments in 'Rock The Casbah' and 'Should I Stay Or Should I Go'. But deep down the band was falling apart under the pressures of success and the competing expectations of idealism and commerce. At one point Joe Strummer simply disappeared for a month, giving rise to lurid rumours of madness or suicide. Topper Headon left after what was tersely described as 'a difference of political direction'. In 1983 Mick Jones, the effective founder and the musical heart of the group, was sacked by Strummer and Simonon. The remaining pair struggled on for a while, using new members, but The Clash's output fizzled out with a poor final album with the less-than-stirring name of 'Cut The Crap'.

Since 1985 The Clash's main personnel have all recorded again. Topper Headon had a brief solo career; Mick Jones formed Big Audio Dynamite; Joe Strummer has done some acting, performed solo, formed a band called Latino Rockabilly War and performed with the Pogues in place of Shane MacGowan; Paul Simonon had a spell with Havana 3am and then returned to painting. Nothing, of

course, has matched The Clash in either scale or prestige. And yet, unlike the Sex Pistols, they have so far resisted the inevitably lucrative invitations to reform for live dates or records. Interest in the band has never disappeared, and was revived dramatically in 1991 when a Levi's jeans ad deployed 'Should I Stay Or Should I Go', thus propelling the band to their sole Number 1 hit in the UK. The irony of a Clash song selling anything, let alone such an iconic item of US capitalism, was not lost on the former members: typically they quarrelled over the issue, with Jones (whose song it was) allowing Levi's to go ahead. An even stranger instance of posthumous Clash controversy occurred a year earlier, when Allied forces first squared up to Iraq before the Gulf War: the song their radio network opened on was 'Rock The Casbah'. . . .

Even in the afterlife, then, The Clash have been a glorious muddle. They could have ended in a blaze of glory, but instead they faded ignominiously. They could, with a hefty dose of willpower, have consolidated their popularity and become a long-running rock institution. But that was not their style either. Somehow, all their human fallibility makes them more endearing. They failed to change the world, or even the music business – the latter, in fact, survived the band's onslaught to see out the Eighties as a more ruthlessly corporate entity than ever before. But there is an unquenchable spirit to The Clash's best music that can still move listeners today. From the young Paul Weller (a punk contemporary who found his own voice with The Jam by following The Clash's example in writing about real life) to the Manic Street Preachers, other musicians have drawn inspiration from The Clash's impassioned urge to make music that mattered. And, in the end, The Clash were for their audience more than they were against anything else. There was an old song entitled 'I Fought The Law And The Law Won' and it seems inevitable that The Clash should have covered it. The words are practically their epitaph. But in the white-hot rush of their noble, naïve, hopeless optimism, The Clash accomplished more than a million clever, cynical, calculating counterparts could ever do.

Paul Du Noyer

ANGRY YOUNG MEN

From the start, The Clash made it clear that politics was part of the package they were offering, whether by the slogans on their clothes or their statements to the press. Of course that meant they were laying themselves open to accusations of hypocrisy and selling-out, but all that came with the territory. The band dated their politicisation from August 1976, when they were caught up in the riots during London's Notting Hill Carnival, but for sceptics there was a niggling doubt. None of the band had a track record of political interest or activism and the cynical suggestion could be made that three arts students (Strummer, Jones and Simonon) and their cohorts had acquired political attitude as a convenient, complementary fashion to the mood of 1976. As their manager was Bernie Rhodes, a man who'd been to the Malcolm McLaren school of punk band packaging, that doubt might be especially amplified. However their supporters – certainly in the first few years – didn't see it that way. When NME, virtually The Clash's house newspaper, published a supplement called The Book Of Modern Music in 1978, they described the band as 'using pop media to perpetuate radical political views, a cross between the

Monkees and the Red Brigade, definitely the new MC5' in a reference to the Detroit band whose sloganising music had been dubbed 'guerrilla rock'. It was a perception The Clash had been happy to promote in the beginning, but by the end they were shying away from it. In the early Eighties The Clash tried to stop the film Rude Boy *being released: it featured footage of them headlining a Rock Against Racism festival and they were concerned it might make them look too political. . . .*

We're anti-fascist, anti-violence, anti-racist. We're against ignorance.

Joe Strummer

25

By the summer and autumn of 1976, the punk movement was well into its stride, although the national media only really picked up on its existence – and its news potential – courtesy of the Sex Pistols's infamous appearance on Bill Grundy's Thames TV show, which sparked off a storm of tabloid outrage. To differentiate themselves from the Pistols's stance of pure anarchy, The Clash's political angle provided the press with a convenient handle.

We know the blacks've got their thing sewn up. They got their own culture, but the young white kids don't have nothing.
Mick Jones, *NME,* 1976

26

I vote for the weirdo, I vote
for the loonies, I vote for
the people off the left wall,
I vote for the individuals.
Joe Strummer

It's not politics –
just the difference
between right and wrong.
Paul Simonon

The Clash are interested in
politics rather than
revolution. Revolution sets a
country back a hundred
years. Revolution is very,
very dangerous. I don't think
we ever were revolutionary. I
think we were always
interested in the politics of
the situation. And I think we
still are. But I think that
England's less interested.
Clash manager, **Bernie Rhodes,**
NME, 1981

Whatever clouds might hang over the band's political posture, there was no question about the total commitment they displayed in live performance. At their first London appearance, a showcase for the music press, one of the journalists present, (Sounds' Giovanni Dadomo) described the impact as 'like being hit by a runaway fire engine'. Bassist Paul Simonon may not have touched a bass before he joined the band, but any lack of technical skill could be overcome by sheer passion and attack.

The Clash taking the stage was like an injection of electricity into the smoky air. They charged headlong into 'White Riot' with shattering energy, strutting and leaping like clockwork robots out of control.

Kris Needs, *Zigzag, 1977*

The Clash played sets of such emotional intensity and heartbursting velocity that all previous convictions (even about punk) were slashed to shredded slivers.

Danny Kelly, *NME, 1986*

'It's that 'White Riot' that gets 'em up every time', growls one of the roadies after the set's conclusion, which tonight, like every other time, draws the front row of kids onto the stage itself on instinct – as though they were being physically impelled there by some perverse form of suction.

Nick Kent, *NME, 1978*

MoDERN iCoNS ●–THE CLASH

The Clash's political message, once released into the public domain, could never be controlled as neatly as a press interview. Their first single 'White Riot' caused particular confusion. Written in September 1976 after the band had witnessed that year's Notting Hill riots, its release unfortunately coincided with a surge in support for the National Front, and some listeners misunderstood the song as a piece of fascist propaganda. The band refuted this: their intention had been to show that whites should take a lead from the black rioters who were prepared to fight to solve their problems. Fans who took certain lyrics and statements at face value simply ended up depressing Strummer and co. In any case, there were always plenty of cynics around to question just how genuine the band's stance had ever been.

Some dimwits accused us of being fascist. Really it's saying that white people are so fucked up and intellectual that they can't seem to get any unified thing together.
Joe Strummer, *Melody Maker,* 1988, on 'White Riot'

I was emotionally shattered . . . completely disheartened to see what's happened to the seeds of what we've planted. If those pricks and kids like them are the fruits of our labours, then they're much worse than those people they were meant to replace.

Joe Strummer, *NME,* May 1980, after seeing violent audiences at a series of gigs in Europe

The thing that pisses me off about the Clashes and Billy Braggs is that all they ever do is state the bleedin' obvious. All Billy Bragg's doing is telling people that Thatcher's a cow. Well, I think most people know that, don't they?!

Rat Scabies, The Damned, 1985

I don't know why people are talking about The Clash being a political band. I didn't know who the Prime Minister was until a couple of weeks ago.

Paul Simonon, 1976

I don't think I'd make such a great rioter . . . .

Mick Jones, *NME,* 1981

WE ARE THE CLASH

. . . .

The Clash was born from an unlikely marriage between New York glam and London pub rock. Mick Jones, after the usual teenage musician's round of short-lived bands, had formed the London SS with Tony James, Billy Idol's future partner in Generation X. The London SS were strongly influenced by the New York Dolls, MC5, the Stooges and the new wave of NYC bands like Television, the Ramones and the Patti Smith Group. Although the band never actually got round to performing, they rehearsed extensively and auditioned widely. Among the musicians Jones encountered along the way were Paul Simonon, Rat Scabies and Topper Headon. He also came across Bernie Rhodes, erstwhile acolyte of T. Rex, some time motor trader, and part of the coterie based around Malcolm McLaren's shops Let It Rock and Sex. Unable to participate fully in the Sex Pistols adventure, courtesy of McLaren's overweening dominance, Bernie Rhodes began working with Jones to develop something out of the remains of the London SS. It was Bernie Rhodes who remembered the good-looking Paul Simonon, who'd auditioned as a vocalist, and suggested he should be recruited as bassist. To fill the vacancy for a vocalist, they turned to Joe Strummer, who had been building up a strong reputation with his R&B pub rock outfit the 101'ers. The Clash legend has it that Strummer chanced across Simonon and Jones in Portobello Road,

but the magical moment is sadly apocryphal. Nonetheless, Strummer was approached to join The Clash. As Strummer had recently shared the bill with the Sex Pistols, who had impressed him hugely, he didn't need too much convincing to join The Clash, although it was a gamble for him. For the unknown band it was a great coup to secure a name vocalist and within a matter of weeks, The Clash were ready to perform at their first gig – supporting the Sex Pistols at the Black Swan, Sheffield, 4 July 1976.

Yesterday I thought I was a crud, then I saw the Sex Pistols and I became a King and decided to move into the future. As soon as I saw them I knew that rhythm and blues was dead.

Joe Strummer, the day he quit the 101'ers, April 1976

33

Although he sometimes denied it, Mick Jones had plenty of guitar heroes. The first album he bought was Cream's 'Disraeli Gears', and during his formative musical years, he styled himself variously on Mott The Hoople's Ian Hunter, Keith Richards and Bowie guitarist Mick Ronson. When Jones discovered the New York Dolls, the final element fell into place for his pre-Clash persona, lived out through his first bands, the Delinquents and the London SS.

When I was sixteen, I had two choices – football or rock. I chose rock because it was less limiting. And it was more exciting and I got into music at a very early age. I went to my first rock concert when I was twelve. It was free, in Hyde Park, and the Nice, Traffic, Junior's Eyes and the Pretty Things were playing.
Mick Jones

A good guitar solo in the right place, a little bit of tension added to the show – there's nothing wrong with having respect for the stage, because you're also out there entertaining.
Mick Jones, *NME,* 1981

I don't believe in guitar heroes. If I walk out to the front of the stage it's because I wanna reach the audience, I want to *communicate* with them. I don't want them to suck my guitar off.
Mick Jones, 1977

Joe Strummer has suffered throughout his career from the tag of 'public schoolboy', which is a touch unfair. He did attend a boarding school, but his father was a clerk in the diplomatic service whose postings took him abroad much of the time, leaving little choice about schooling. The archetypal public schoolboy he is not, though he certainly didn't come from a deprived background. It was at boarding school that he first heard the Stones's 'Not Fade Away'. This started him along the road that led via folk-rock at art school, where he called himself Woody after Woody Guthrie, to R&B with the 101'ers, whose pub-rock success brought the charismatic Woody, now calling himself Joe Strummer, to the attention of the embryonic Clash.

It's the only thing that's living to me.
I shall live and die and be judged by it.
Joe Strummer, *Sounds,* 1988, on rock'n'roll

With Joe I could see he was a great
performer saddled with a duff band.
Mick Jones, *NME,* 1978

I've read everything that T. E. Lawrence
wrote, he was my hero.
Joe Strummer

I ain't gonna fuck myself
up like I seen those other
guys fuck themselves up.
Keeping all their money
for themselves and getting
into their heads, and
thinking they're the
greatest. I've planned
what I'm gonna do with
my money if it happens.
Secret plans.

Joe Strummer, 1977

The classic Clash rhythm section of Simonon and Headon brought together two musicians from the opposite ends of musical experience – maybe that's what made it click. Paul Simonon, the third art school student, whose talents as a painter would be re-awakened after The Clash split, was picked as the band's bassist primarily for his looks, since he'd never played before: in the true spirit of punk, he learned the basics in a few days. Topper Headon took over as drummer in 1977 after recordings for the first album had been completed by Terry Chimes from the original line-up. He had already toured abroad, doing the rounds of US bases in Germany.

I always wanted to be a guitarist, not a bass player, but because I couldn't play nothing – I just used to leap about with it and not hit any right notes – so in the end I thought 'I'll be the bass player – but I'll be the best bass player'.

Paul Simonon

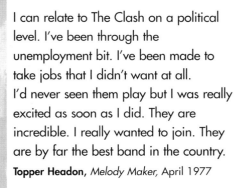

I can relate to The Clash on a political level. I've been through the unemployment bit. I've been made to take jobs that I didn't want at all. I'd never seen them play but I was really excited as soon as I did. They are incredible. I really wanted to join. They are by far the best band in the country.

Topper Headon, *Melody Maker,* April 1977

I was the dark horse of The Clash. If anybody'd ever said to me, in an interview, 'What do you do with your spare time?' maybe I'd have turned around and given them a big art lecture. But I think they thought I was an idiot . . . a thicko from south London.

Paul Simonon, *Melody Maker,* 1989

The ensemble sound surges forth in raging fettle, gorgeous power chord structures welded to Topper Headon's devilishly incisive drumming and Paul Simonon's kamikaze bassline.

Nick Kent, *NME,* 1978, on 'Give 'Em Enough Rope'

PERFECTING THE PACKAGE

∙ ∙

The political attitude and the raw energy of the music that The Clash purveyed to the punters of 1976 was topped off by the perfection of the name and the studied choice of garb. When Joe Strummer's 101'ers had been supported by the Sex Pistols, he had been particularly struck by Malcolm McLaren's attention to sartorial detail. It was important for The Clash to establish a different look to the Pistols, who benefited from the fact that McLaren could kit them out from his own shop. The early Clash image was a cross between the Patti Smith Group and a spare mod feel – a style that particularly suited Paul Simonon, who had the right cool and the requisite credibility: a broken family background, a period as a skinhead while he'd been at school. Simonon it was who came up with the band name: early versions had included the Phones and the Mirrors, the Psychotic Negatives and the Weak Heart Drops. None lasted long. Paul found the word 'clash' cropping up frequently in the pages of the Evening Standard *– and his suggestion was taken up by the rest of the band who liked its energy and confrontational directness. For their first showcase performance in their rehearsal room, the walls, amps and speakers were painted pink and black, Simonon created an urban landscape mural, and the band spattered paint over their clothes. By the end of 1976, after the band had hardened up their political profile, that approach had developed into*

a uniform of boiler suits, covered with patches of colour and stencilled slogans: taken from reggae records, 'UNDER HEAVY MANNERS', 'HEAVY DUTY DISCIPLINE'; from their own lyrics and song titles, 'KNIVES IN W11', 'WHITE RIOT', 'STEN GUNS IN KNIGHTSBRIDGE'; or to make a personal point – Strummer's boiler suit carried the legend, 'CHUCK BERRY IS DEAD' to show he'd rejected his R&B past. The urban guerrillas had found their look.

Onomatopoeically violent and glowering portentous, it seemed to grab the '70s by the lapels and threaten its dreary life with mad-eyed damage.

Danny Kelly, *NME,*
1986, on The Clash's name

41

The urban look was a perfect match with The Clash's core stamping ground: the W11 area of London. Their area encompassed the downtrodden districts of Ladbroke Grove and Shepherd's Bush, wallowing amid oppressing, depressing tower blocks overlooking the Westway overpass and scything out through the sprawl of West London. Paul Simonon painted a mural of the scene in their first rehearsal room: against this 'London's Burning' backdrop of decline and decay, The Clash could project the siege mentality of a Baader-Meinhof cell, a gang identity that helped bond them together.

We love the place – blocks of flats, concrete. I hate the country. The minute I see cows I get sick.
Joe Strummer, *Zigzag, 1977,* on London

With the Stones it was drugs and knives; with The Clash it's all guns and guerillas. All Rock Bands For Boys pick the paraphernalia of image with care and The Clash do it monstrously well, cover their bases with such cunning, take upon themselves the lustre of an irresistible force to such an extent that even mildly pointing out that this would be a better record if you could actually hear what Strummer is singing about without consulting the lyrics on the sleeve somehow sounds almost fascist.

Dave Hepworth, *Sounds*, 1979, on 'English Civil War'

We ain't no urban guerrilla outfit. Our gunpower is strictly limited. All we want to achieve is an atmosphere where things can happen. We want to keep the spirit of the free world. We want to keep *out* that safe, soapy slush that comes out of the radio.

Joe Strummer

MoDERN iCoNS ●–THE CLASH

Whether the look and the stance was calculated, it didn't really matter – there was nowhere for The Clash's music to hide. Punk did not allow for carefully blended, beautifully balanced soundscapes hiding a multitude of sins. If it wasn't in your face, then it wasn't happening. Joe Strummer was exhilarated at his very first rehearsal by the looseness, the abandon that his new bandmates possessed. By 'London Calling' and 'Sandinista!' other influences were diluting the punk sound, but even so the band felt they had managed to retain their original energy.

We're not afraid to play around. What we're doing now is experimenting. But I'll only put it on a record if it's worth listening to.
Joe Strummer, *NME,* on 'Sandinista!'

Everything has been reduced to an insignia. The Clash's rock'n'roll is primordial not in the way of rockabilly (because they never ever swing like rockabilly does and on the supercharged ignition of 'Brand New Cadillac' traditional rock'n'roll is moonshot, revved up) but in the blunt anger of the simplest figure or rhythm hammered on a line of deadeye consistency.
Richard Cook, Brixton, *NME,* 1982, on The Clash at the Fair Deal

It only takes an hour to write a song. You can play everything inside of three weeks. Everyone knows it's dead easy.
Joe Strummer

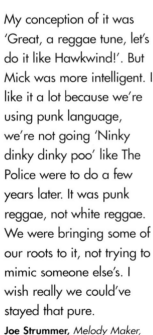

My conception of it was
'Great, a reggae tune, let's
do it like Hawkwind!'. But
Mick was more intelligent. I
like it a lot because we're
using punk language,
we're not going 'Ninky
dinky dinky poo' like The
Police were to do a few
years later. It was punk
reggae, not white reggae.
We were bringing some of
our roots to it, not trying to
mimic someone else's. I
wish really we could've
stayed that pure.

Joe Strummer, *Melody Maker,*
1988, on 'Police And Thieves'

MoDERN iCoNS ●-THE CLASH

Considering the band's initial commitment to the basics of the punk image, they displayed a realistic attitude to adapting themselves for a changing market. As other punk bands fell by the wayside, The Clash not only survived relatively intact into the Eighties but were the only classic punk outfit to crack the States. On their first tour they didn't make it easy for themselves, calling it 'The Pearl Harbour 79' tour, and opening each set with 'I'm So Bored With the USA', but they hit a nerve – liggers from Andy Warhol to Robert de Niro came to the gigs. And the band responded to America, a love affair with the country that affected their image and their sound.

You'll be glad to know that The Clash's 'Give 'Em Enough Rope' album has been safely released in the States, and that it's identical to the UK edition except that 'All The Young Punks' has been mysteriously mistitled on the sleeve. Could it be that CBS US didn't want the word 'punk' to put any radio stations off playing the album . . . .
NME, 1978

46

We don't walk around with green hair and bondage trousers anymore. We just want to look, sort of, flash these days.
Joe Strummer, 1979

We wanted to see America. It wasn't entirely successful. I kept falling asleep, it was a long drive.
Mick Jones

Here they have a tendency to lay money on the stage instead of gobbing. I made 17 dollars the other day – it's great!
Paul Simonon, *NME,*
1979, on US audiences

It's easier when there's no spit on the guitar – it gets slippery. The only people who gob in England are up north – they're a bit behind.
Mick Jones, *NME,* 1979

PUNKADELIC

. . . .

Although the Sex Pistols were already up and running by the time
The Clash emerged in the spring and summer of 1976, they became
part of the punk movement early enough to become an essential part
of its growth, appearing at seminal events like the 100 Club's Punk
Festival in September 1976. Along with the Pistols, they were out
there encouraging their fans to take their lead and start up their own
bands. In the wake of each date, a clutch of new punk bands
heeded their advice – get a guitar, just start playing, play what you
feel, let the anger out. In the same way, the Sniffing Glue *fanzine*
spawned an alternative music press which kept pressure on the
name bands not to lose sight of punk ideals. Fans could crash out in
the bands's hotel rooms: it was the kind of contact and connection
that the supergroup stadium acts had forgotten, or chosen to ignore.
But the punk scene was not one glorious tale of camaraderie. From
the outset there was rivalry between the bands, a level of squabbling
that often blew over as quickly as it lingered and festered, but which
the music press took delight in whipping up whenever possible. In
the case of the Pistols and The Clash, there was an extra edge from
the relationship between Malcolm McLaren and Bernie Rhodes, who
had worked with McLaren while the Pistols were coming into
existence. Some reports suggested it was Rhodes who'd discovered
Johnny Rotten. McLaren always liked to claim that the Pistols were
the Number One band. It all added piquancy to events.

I think they're the first band to come along who'll really frighten the Sex Pistols shitless.

Giovanni Dadomo, *Sounds,* 1976

The Clash hit the ground running. The speed with which they absorbed Joe Strummer into their ranks gave them the momentum they needed. There had been no time for the excitement and the energy of the first rehearsals to become dissipated. The time was ripe, and the timing was impeccable. Within the space of a few gigs they had found an audience who understood what they were all about.

'The Clash are coming' . . . The Clash . . . The Clash . . . The Clash . . . The Clash . . . In the late summer London of 1976 it wasn't easy to avoid those two words – snowflakes in a blizzard of fevered, word-of-mouth anticipation.
Danny Kelly, *NME,* 1986

It's about sheer boredom, it meant that London was burning with frustration. The city felt alive to us, we could feel that the punk scene was just burning open at that time. It was a great summer that.
Joe Strummer, *Melody Maker,* 1988, on 'London's Burning'

Even more than anything the Pistols ever did, The Clash's first album was to epitomize the punk stereotype. What were later to become clichés were, at the time, angry young innovations.
NME, 1978

MoDERN iCoNS ●- THE CLASH

Supporting the Sex Pistols on their 'Anarchy' tour of December 1976 was a turbulent round of cancelled gigs, as the Pistols's antics with Bill Grundy on national TV had led to shock-horror headlines in the tabloid press and in turn to local councils wringing their hands in consternation. The press came along to sniff out more outrage and atrocity, and The Clash had to spend most of the time cooped up in their hotel, unable to escape and find their fans.

All that business on the Pistols tour! I hated it. I HATED it. It was the Pistols time. We were in the background. The first few nights were terrible. We were just locked up in the hotel room with the Pistols doing nothing.

Joe Strummer, *Melody Maker,* on the 1976 'Anarchy' tour

There was this time when that feeling of being second-best was really getting to us. And, of course, Malcolm would help it along by throwing in some story like, oh Christ, there was this time when we heard that the Pistols had come over had nicked some of our gear, as a gesture of contempt, so to speak. So we'd be immediately up in arms . . . like y'know, 'let's get 'em, let's go over to their rehearsal place and rip off their microphones', always something petty.
Mick Jones, *NME,* 1978

This stuff about fans staying in our hotel rooms and coming backstage is very important – the responsibility is to the fans, not only to keep in touch but also to show that we do care, and I believe that this group cares more than any other in the country.
Mick Jones, *Melody Maker,* July 1978

There may not have been anything to take the place of punk, but inevitably the passion and the purpose of the first two years had to lose its focus. Acts like the Stranglers and the Jam were revealing their pop leanings. Second-wave punk bands like the Adverts were charting with tasteless ('Gary Gilmore's Eyes') but perfectly palatable singles. New wave bands from the States were arriving in town. And the bands who'd created it all were splitting up – by spring 1978 The Clash had seen the break-up of the Damned, the Heartbreakers and, above all, the Pistols.

It ain't punk. It ain't new wave. It's the next step, and the logical progression for groups to move. Call it what you like – all the terms stink. Just call it rock'n'roll.
Mick Jones, 1977

It made us feel lonely, somehow. There was nothing to chase.
Paul Simonon, *Melody Maker, 1978,* on the break-up of the Sex Pistols

Everyone is making out that punk is old-fashioned, but it doesn't look as if anything important has taken over from it. Joe was one of the people who came up with punk and he's been through the whole thing, so if people are going to turn around and blow him out they'd better make sure there's someone better to take his place.
Bernie Rhodes, *NME,* 1982

Punk's now become 'Oh yeah, he's got zips all over him sewed on by his mother and he's shouting in Cockney, making no attempt to sing from the heart and the guitarist is deliberately playing monotonously, and they're all playing as fast as possible, so this is punk, so yeah, I can dig this!'. There are some people who are becoming snobs.

Mick Jones, *NME*

55

THE ROUGH AND THE SMOOTH

When punk started, the big record companies weren't interested. It was left to the small independents, with Stiff and Chiswick at the forefront, to sign up bands. Once the music press coverage, the national media exposure and the prospect of some decent sales figures reached the attention of the key players in the major labels, competition to pick up the top bands flourished. The Sex Pistols enjoyed the favours of EMI, their first port of call, until the label dropped them in January 1977, due to adverse publicity. In March 1977 they signed with A&M – only to be fired six days later. Finally they signed with Virgin. (The ever-astute McLaren made money on every deal.) The Vibrators went to RAK, the Stranglers got a deal with United Artists, but The Clash were still waiting. Chris Parry of Polydor, who'd missed on the Pistols, arranged for the band to record some demos in November 1976, with Guy Stevens, a name producer with a reputation for wild behaviour. Further demos were recorded in early 1977, as no deal had been forthcoming, and Chris Parry finally convinced Polydor to make an offer of £25,000. Then, at the last minute, Bernie Rhodes struck a deal with Maurice Oberstein at CBS. Polydor recovered from the blow and signed The Jam for a snip of the £100,000 Clash/CBS deal. When the news broke, fans and critics alike reacted badly – this was a sell-out. Although it was undoubtedly a major deal in terms of the other punk

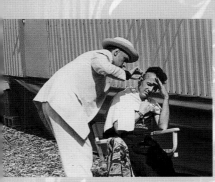

bands at the time, and a tribute to Bernie Rhodes's skill in hustling, the cash didn't go far. Tour costs and equipment ate into most of it. Yet, however much the band and its management justified the logic of signing with a major label to get their music and their message to as wide an audience as possible, the stigma stuck, along with the accusations of cosying up to the establishment.

Punk died the day
The Clash signed to CBS.
Mark P., *Sniffin' Glue*

Trite it may be, but it's true that you can't please all the people all of the time. If you're a band setting out with lofty ideals, claiming a politically correct high ground, then the backlash will never be long in arriving. The Clash found that out many a time.

Let's talk about fucking Joe Strummer. When he went missing that time and they cancelled the tour, they found him in parlez-vous Français having a holiday with a young kitty. How lovely! Joe, the kids are where it's at, right?! Hypocrite.
Johnny Rotten, 1982, on Joe Strummer's 'disappearance'

The Clash are a bunch of clapped-out old social workers.
Fred and **Judy Vermorel,** Sex Pistols biographers, 1978

People like The Clash always said they wouldn't do it, but . . . to even be in something as corrupt as the music business is far worse than doing something stupid like *Top Of The Pops.*
Pete Wylie, 1983

A joyless, emotionless, directionless, self-important music, something like a shambolic HM quartet converted to Mao minutes before a show but still retaining the original ego-pushy set, swaggers and all.
Ian Penman, *NME,* 1978

The 1977 deal with CBS was down to Bernie Rhodes. Sacked as their manager the following year, he returned just over two years later to oversee the band's last years. Without his influence, there most likely would have been no Clash, even if his wish for control, to be a master puppeteer in the McLaren mould, led to friction, notably with Mick Jones.

His presence was felt in everything, in every part of the whole movie, you know. He would spend hours visionising the backdrop of the stage set, the T-shirts, the posters. Bernie also gave us our direction: he told us to write about what affects us as *we* live. In a lot of ways we were young and stupid then.

Joe Strummer, *Q* magazine, 1990, on Bernie Rhodes

He's a difficult bloke to deal with. He's very paranoid. He's always into money, although he pretends not to be. People find it difficult to relate to Bernie.

Anonymous record executive, *NME,* 1978

We fell out with Bernie, he lost control of us, and it's a pity because we made a good team.

Joe Strummer, *NME,* 1980

Every situation needs a scapegoat, and I became it.

Bernie Rhodes, *The Face,* 1981

MoDERN iCoNS ● – THE CLASH

In April 1982, Joe Strummer went AWOL on the eve of a 19-date tour of the UK. Tour dates were postponed and speculation was rife. Was it a publicity stunt dreamt up by Bernie Rhodes, or had the pressure and the stress got too much? Strummer's subsequent interviews over the years suggested an element of both. Whatever the reality, his vanishing act marked the beginning of the end for The Clash.

Joe's personal conflict is – where does the socially concerned rock artist stand in the bubblegum environment of today? I think he's probably gone away for a serious re-think. I think Joe has just gone away to examine what it is all about. We've got to find this bloke. He'll get a bollocking when he gets back, but it's still better that he comes back.

Bernie Rhodes, *NME,* 1982

THE ROUGH AND THE SMOOTH

The fact that he went just cleared the air and made you realise more of where you stood individually as well as to two or three other people. I knew he was coming back.
Paul Simonon, *NME,* 1982, on Joe's runner

I went to shake The Clash up, to shake The Clash fans up, to shake The Clash haters up, and to shake myself up too.
Joe Strummer, *Sounds,* 1982

When this was recorded none of us were really talking to each other so I suppose its title is horribly appropriate in terms of how I felt at the time.
Paul Simonon, *Melody Maker,* 1988, on 1982's 'Should I Stay Or Should I Go'

MUSICAL MOMENTS

Joe Strummer had a theory why The Clash were the only one of the London punk bands to find any real success in the notoriously resistant American market. He put it all down to the blend of influences that each member brought to the band. As a teenager he had been immersed in blues and English R&B before going back to black American R&B. Mick Jones had caught some of the same sounds, but had added on an additional dimension: the glam/trash scene fronted by the New York Dolls and Iggy Pop's Stooges. Behind the two guitarists Topper Headon had learnt his trade on what Strummer called the 'soul/chicken-in-the-basket' circuit, and the soul licks were deep in his system. And Paul Simonon, well he had the unique style that came from self-instruction, but he had soul too – 'even the best bassists in the world didn't express so much soul.' Simonon himself claimed that the first live rock'n'roll he'd encountered was when he went to a Sex Pistols gig. Before that he'd only listened to bluebeat and ska at the Streatham Locarno. Any blues and soul were submerged deep down in the mix on the band's first album, which for many listeners and reviewers, was a defining encapsulation of the punk sound and the punk movement. When the second album, 'Give 'Em Enough Rope', was released, critical opinion, particularly in retrospect, was that the verve and attack of 'The Clash' had grown stale and stereotyped. 'London Calling' was

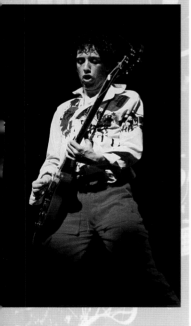

the first attempt to absorb all the music they'd listened to and create a distinct hybrid – it worked so well for the American market that the editors of Rolling Stone *voted it the best album of the Eighties. After a panning over the sprawl of 'Sandinista!', the band re-established some kind of resolution of the contradiction between punk instincts and Americana – leaning heavily towards the commercial with 'Rock The Casbah' and 'Should I Stay' on 'Combat Rock', the last album before The Clash as known and loved began to unravel.*

I suppose my main influences are Mott The Hoople, The Kinks and The Stones, but I just stopped believing.
Mick Jones

'The Clash' was released in April 1977, recorded in a blitz of three 3-day sessions that February. The whole album was wrapped up by the first week of March, and pushed out by CBS – this was the New Thing, and speed was of the essence. But along the way, despite the rush, the CBS in-house design team created a classic to accompany the corruscating music it contained.

I can't mince words here. I've only heard it once, but I know this is the most exciting album I've heard in years. I can't think about it for more than a minute without feeling like I'm going to explode.

It's captured the essence of The Clash. Their intense conviction is here in all its blazing glory.

Kris Needs, *Zigzag,* 1977

The Clash album is like a mirror. It reflects all the shit. It shows us the truth.

Mark Perry, *Sniffin' Glue* editor, 1977

'The Clash' was everything that 'Bollocks' promised but wasn't; was terrifyingly ferocious, but repeatedly, sometimes deliberately, hilarious; was the most accurate time-capsule snapshot of Britain in '77; and was an opening blast so singlemindedly *engaged* and recklessly *energised* that it borders on the insane.

Danny Kelly, *NME,* 1986

By the time 'London Calling' came out, the Sex Pistols had imploded. The band had expanded their range, to the scorn of the punk fundamentalists, who thought that The Clash, their Clash, were now becoming just another band.

With 'London Calling' it wasn't *all* apples and roses. The press dug it but there was a very heavy purist lobby going at the time who were saying it wasn't 'punk' and that it was deliberately designed to appeal to American radio. I just *laughed*, you know, because we made that album in a grimy room in Pimlico.

Joe Strummer, *Q* magazine, 1990

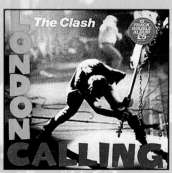

Despite the trimming and the compromises, their music remains a crackling live wire that can't be silenced. And anyone in America who still cares about rock'n'roll must listen.
Tom Carson, *Rolling Stone,* 1980

The Clash have discovered America and, by the same process, themselves.
James Truman, *Melody Maker,* 1979

We recorded the tracks for 'London Calling', then went on a tour of America while Guy Stevens and Bill Price mixed it. And they sent a cassette over. And we were all driving to Monterey, all four of us in a minivan, hearing 'London Calling' back for the first time on the van stereo. That felt pretty good, riding down that road in the dark . . . .
Joe Strummer, *Q* magazine, 1990

69

MoDERN iCoNS ●-THE CLASH

At the end of the recording sessions for 'Sandinista!', the band found they had far too many tracks for a double album. The solution was simple: make it a triple album. These had usually been the indulgence of rambling, grandiose progressive rock acts: The Clash overcame that by maintaining punk's insistence on value for money and demanding that CBS issue the album at the same price as a single LP – a fiver. A deal was struck only when the band agreed to forgo royalties on the first 200,000 copies sold. Their principled stand failed: they never even got close to selling 200,000.

We'd just gotten off an American tour
and that was recorded in like a three-
week burst in Electric Ladyland in New
York. We hadn't written it, we just booked
the time and went straight in and made it
up as we were going along.

Joe Strummer, *Q* magazine, 1990

The Clash have become a messy
conglomerate of present-day Don Quixotes.
So credible, so concerned, and so in control
of their output, that from behind a mixing
desk, they can now tilt at more non-existent
windmills than even the Pentagon is aware of.

John Shearlaw, *Record Mirror,* 1980

This record is strong testimony that The
Clash have – temporarily at least – lost a
grip on their bearings and find
themselves parked in a cul de sac.

Nick Kent, *NME,* 1980

Listen, the bottom line on 'Sandinista!' is that
you can dance all the way through it. The only
thing is that you have to dance a certain way.

Mick Jones

CLASH POINT

The ending of The Clash should have been a glorious explosion, or a dignified departure, sadly it was neither. Like a family in the throes of an over-extended divorce, the last three years of the band were a lingering tale of bad feelings, carping remarks, and unremarkable music. The die was cast when Joe Strummer returned from his impromptu disappearance in April and May of 1982. By the time he had rejoined the fold, Topper Headon was out on his ear, the victim of drug problems which would dog the drummer after he'd left, ending in a 15-month jail sentence later in the decade. A number of possible returns to the music business, including a solo album, came to nothing. Eighteen months later, Mick Jones had gone too. Simmering resentments within the band had come to a head over a three-day festival in Los Angeles, organised by Steve Wozniak of Apple computers. There were arguments about the substantial money involved – The Clash had been offered half a million dollars to appear and had kicked up an almighty fuss about ticket prices, forcing the promoters and other bands to donate a proportion of their earnings to worthy causes. It was all symptomatic of a deeper malaise. Strummer and Simonon wanted to return to the basic of punk. Jones wanted to move on, as he would with Big Audio Dynamite. Strummer wanted to go out on the road. Jones wanted to take time off. And that was that. Strummer and Simonon limped on with some new recruits, but by 1985 the game was up.

72

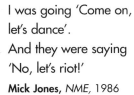

I was going 'Come on, let's dance'.
And they were saying 'No, let's riot!'
Mick Jones, *NME,* 1986

The official press statements gave little away when Headon and Jones were booted out. There was plenty of mud-slinging in the subsequent years, primarily in Jones's direction. They'd forgotten the Baader-Meinhof gang togetherness of the early days, but as time passed the anger mellowed.

It was his decision. I think he felt it's not too easy to be in The Clash, it's not as simple as being in a comfortable, we're-just-entertainers group, and he wanted to do that, just play music.

Joe Strummer, *NME,* 1982, on Topper leaving

Joe Strummer and Paul Simonon have decided that Mick Jones should leave the group. It is felt that Jones has drifted apart from the original idea of The Clash. In future, it will allow Joe and Paul to get on with the job that Joe and Paul set out to do from the beginning.

Official statement, September 1983

74

If you're in a team you can't go round not trusting members of that team and still remain a part of it with honour. I thought he should've left himself. We only pushed him. He had to go.

Joe Strummer, *NME,* 1984, on Mick Jones

Most groups will stand the regulation English foot apart if you pose them against a wall, but The Clash touch each other all the time. They quarrel a lot, but it's like lovers' quarrels, they're over as soon as they start. Most of the quarrels can be traced back to their laundry anyway!

Photographer **Pennie Smith,** *NME,* 1981

I did him wrong.
I stabbed him in the back. My ego was definitely telling me, "Go on, get rid of him".

Joe Strummer, *NME*

MoDERN iCoNS — THE CLASH

Ever since 1985 rumours of a re-formed Clash have circulated with regularity. The lessons of the Eighties should be learnt. 1976 was a bright, burning moment in time. It shouldn't be resurrected.

After six months playing to 10,000 people you don't connect to real life anymore. That's what happened to the Clash. The meaning of the songs were just too far divorced from the lifestyle. The moment you stop struggling, what's the point? It becomes designer struggle.

Joe Strummer, *Q* magazine, 1988

The Clash rarely came up with the right answer, but they were smart enough and aware enough to ask the right questions. True, they exemplified personality cult, bullshit and posturing and they conned themselves with even more speed-crazed fervour than they conned the public, but once you take bullshit and posturing out of rock'n'roll there isn't exactly a hell of a lot left.

Charles Shaar Murray, *Q* magazine, 1988

To be honest, I wish we were still together today. It was a good band, but the trouble was we fell to ego.

Joe Strummer

THE MUSIC

★★★★★   Essential listening
★★★   OK
★   Frankly, not the best!

SINGLES

White Riot/1977 – March 1977 ★★★★¹/₂
It's pointless to categorise this with the other records: 'White Riot' isn't a poxy single of the week, it's the first meaningful event all year.
Tom Robinson, NME, 1977

Complete Control/The City of The Dead –
    September 1977 ★★★★
Good though the Pistols' singles are, this knife-edged masterwork makes mincemeat of them. Reggae and punk are forever talked of in the same breath . . . Now the relationship has been consummated.
Ian Birch, Melody Maker, 1977

Clash City Rockers/Jail Guitar Doors – February 1978 ★★★¹/₂
Acidic lyrics, great pounding beat. Reached Number 12 in the UK.

(White Man) In Hammersmith Palais/The Prisoner – June 1978 ★★★¹/₂
Though this record contains the basic elements-to-turn-the-tables, as producers The Clash sell themselves far short of their obvious potential . . . . There's absolutely nothing wrong with The Clash that a good producer couldn't rectify.
Roy Carr, NME, 1978

Tommy Gun/1-2, Crush On You – November 1978 ★★★
Less raw than 'White Riot', 'Tommy Gun' was the band's first Top 20 hit in the UK.

English Civil War/Pressure Drop – February 1979 ★★★
The Clash do it monstrously well, cover their bases with such cunning, take upon themselves the lustre of an irresistible force . . . .
Dave Hepworth, Sounds1979

London Calling/Armagideon Time – December 1979 ★★★★½
*An irresistibly rolling gait, finely underplayed performances and sweet harmonies
on the title words. The lyrics are still apocalyptic clarion calls, but now Joe sings
them with a natural assurance and clarity that make them much more forceful.*
Ian Birch, *Melody Maker,* 1979

Bankrobber/Rockers Galore... UK Tour – July 1980 ★★★★
Excellent white reggae. Reached Number 12 in the UK.

The Magnificent Seven/The Magnificent Dance – April 1981 ★★★½
*A great record. It features a superb bassline, an intelligent lyric, and succeeds
beautifully because Joe Strummer understands that the rhythm of his words
are just as important as Mick Jones' funk guitar.*
Paolo Hewitt, *Melody Maker,* 1981

This Is Radio Clash/Radio Clash – December 1981 ★★★
*A sprawling, splintered fantasy which presents the zombified
vision of would-be media guerrillas with rampant hysteria.*
Gavin Martin, *NME,* 1981

Made it to Number 47 in the UK.

Rock The Casbah/Long Time Jerk – June 1982, re-released April
  1991 ★★★★
*One of their finest moments. Written by Topper Headon, 'Rock
The Casbah' became a worldwide hit (US Top 10 and UK Top
30), shooting The Clash into the American mainstream.*

Should I Stay Or Should I Go/Straight To Hell – September 1982, re-released
  February 1991 ★★★★½
*Though it could well be the rambling Stonesy 'Should I Stay or Should I Go' that
will pick up most of the airplay, it is 'Straight To Hell' that is the reaffirmation that
there is still life in The Clash.*
Adrian Thrills, *NME,* 1982

This Is England/Do It Now – September 1985 ★★½

EP
The Cost Of Living – May 1979 ★★★
I Fought The Law/Groovy Times/Gates Of The West/Capital Radio ★★★★

MoDERN iCoNS●–THE CLASH

ALBUMS

The Clash – April 1977 ★★★★
Janie Jones/Remote Control/I'm So Bored With The U.S.A./White Riot/Hate &
War/What's My Name/Deny/London's Burning/Career
Opportunities/Cheat/Protex Blue/Police & Thieves (or Hate & War)/48
Hours/Garageland
Better than any other punk-rock album, 'The Clash' convincingly vents its outrage
and frustration . . . and backs them with simple, careful, driving rock.
Charley Walters, *Rolling Stone,* 1977

Give 'Em Enough Rope – November 1978 ★★★¹/₂
Safe European Home/English Civil War/Tommy Gun/Julie's Been Working For
The Drug Squad/Last Gang In Town/Guns On The Roof/Drug-stabbing Time/Stay
Free/Cheapskates/All The Young Punks (New Boots And Contracts)
Despite poor sales in the USA – 'Give 'Em Enough Rope' only made it to Number
128 – the album reached Number 2 in the UK charts.

London Calling – December 1979 ★★★★★
London Calling/Brand New Cadillac/Jimmy Jazz/Hateful/Rudie Can't
Fail/Spanish Bombs/The Right Profile/Lost In The
Supermarket/Clampdown/The Guns Of Brixton/
Wrong 'Em Boyo/Death Or Glory/Koka Kola/
The Card Cheat/Lover's Rock/Four Horsemen/I'm
Not Down/Revolution Rock

The Clash love rock'n'roll, which is why they play
it, but they want to live up to its promises, which is
why they play it the way they do. With groups like
The Clash on the case, rock ain't in the cultural
dumper: 'London Calling' makes up for all the bad
rock'n'roll played over the last decade.
Charles Shaar Murray, *NME,* 1978

Sandinista! – December 1980 ★★★
The Magnificent Seven/Hitsville U.K./Junco Partner/Ivan Meets G.I. Joe/The
Leader/Something About England/Rebel Waltz/Look Here/The Crooked

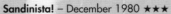

Beat/Somebody Got Murdered/One More Time/One More Dub/Lightning
Strikes (Not Once But Twice)/Up In Heaven (Not Only Here)/Corner Soul/Let's
Go Crazy/If Music Could Talk/The Sound Of The Sinners/Police On My
Back/Midnight Log/The Equaliser/The Call
Up/Washington Bullets/ Broadway/Lose This
Skin/Charlie Don't Surf/Mensforth Hill/Junkie
Slip/ Kingston Advice/The Street Parade/
Version City/Living In Fame/Silicone On
Sapphire/ Version Pardner/Career
Opportunities/ Shepherds Delight
The fourth Clash album is an adventure of
diversity and wit, of struggle and freedom,
of excellence . . . .
Robbi Millar, *Sounds,* 1980
'Sandinista!' was the first Clash album to
sell more copies in the US than the UK.

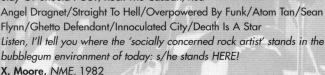

Combat Rock – May 1982 ★★★★
Know Your Rights/Car Jamming/Should I
Stay Or Should I Go?/Rock The Casbah/Red
Angel Dragnet/Straight To Hell/Overpowered By Funk/Atom Tan/Sean
Flynn/Ghetto Defendant/Innoculated City/Death Is A Star
Listen, I'll tell you where the 'socially concerned rock artist' stands in the
bubblegum environment of today: s/he stands HERE!
X. Moore, *NME,* 1982

Cut The Crap – November 1985 ★★
Dictator/Dirty Punk/We Are The Clash/Are You Red...y?/Cool Under
Heat/Movers And Shakers/This Is England/Three Card Trick/Play To
Win/Fingerpoppin'/North And South/Life Is Wild

THE HISTORY

Key Dates

April – June 1976
The Clash emerges from the ashes of the London SS under the
guidance of Mick Jones and manager Bernie Rhodes. They
recruit Paul Simonon, who has never played an instrument in
his life but picks up the rudiments of bass guitar, and persuade
Joe Strummer of pub rock band the 101'ers to join. The band is rounded out by
drummer Terry Chimes and future Public Image Limited guitarist Keith Levene.

4 July 1976
Debut appearance of The Clash: they support the Sex Pistols in Sheffield, less than
a month after the group has started rehearsing together. No formal reviews exist,
but an anonymous letter writer in *Sounds* says 'Clash were just a cacophonous
barrage of noise'.

August 1976
First London performance: a showcase in their Chalk Farm rehearsal room for the
press. Only three attend, but they include *Melody Maker*'s Caroline Coon and
Sounds's Giovanni Dadomo.
At the end of the month The Clash are part of the Midnight Special event at the
Screen on the Green cinema in Islington, and support the Sex Pistols at the 100 Club.

September 1976
The Clash perform at the 100 Club's seminal Punk Festival, alongside the Pistols,
the Damned, the Buzzcocks, Vibrators, Siouxsie and the Banshees, Subway Sect
and French act Stinky Toys.

December 1976
The Clash play on the Sex Pistols's 'Anarchy In The UK' tour – press coverage of
the Pistols and the punk movement mean that the majority of the gigs are
cancelled, and the tour is something of a self-fulfilling shambles. Before the tour
Keith Levene and Terry Chimes have both left The Clash and the drum seat is
taken by Rob Harper.

January 1977
The Clash sign to CBS. Polydor has all but signed them for £25,000, but Bernie Rhodes swops to CBS at the eleventh hour for £100,000.

March 1977
First single 'White Riot' released – drummer Terry Chimes has agreed to sit in on drums for their first recording sessions. The single becomes an instant punk cult classic. The band has a headline gig at the Harlesden Colosseum. Jon Moss, later of Culture Club, is lined up as drummer, but pulls out, and Terry Chimes helps out again.

April 1977
First album 'The Clash' released, enters the charts at Number 12 – recorded in three quick weekend sessions using the soundman as producer. Auditions start for replacement drummer. The story is that 206 drummers are tried out. Nicky 'Topper' Headon gets the nod.

May 1977
The Clash's first major headlining tour, the 'White Riot' tour, with the Jam (who pull out half way through after disagreements over money and sound mixes), the Buzzcocks, Subway Sect and the Slits. The show at the Rainbow, Finsbury Park, London on 9 May is a punk milestone – 'White Riot' leads to fans tearing out 200 seats and throwing the wreckage onstage.

September 1977
The single 'Complete Control' is released, produced by top Jamaican producer Lee Perry. The track is inspired by CBS's decision in May to release 'Remote Control' as The Clash's second single without consulting the band, the first of many skirmishes.

February 1978
Strummer hospitalised with hepatitis: he believes it is from swallowing audience spit during the 'Get Out Of Control' tour in late 1977.

March 1978
While debut album becomes biggest selling imported album in US (racking up over 100,000 copies by the time it is formally released in a revised version by Epic in 1979), Simonon and Headon are arrested for shooting racing pigeons while testing out an air rifle on the roof of their rehearsal rooms.

April 1978
The Clash headline a massive Rock Against Racism rally in London's Victoria Park, along with Tom Robinson, Pete Townshend, the Members and the Pop Group.

July 1978
The Clash hook up with American producer Sandy Pearlman who produces rest of their second album. Strummer and Jones spend three weeks in San Francisco doing overdubs, before travelling around the States.

October 1978
Manager Bernie Rhodes is told his services are no longer required. Tensions have come to a head over a gig at the Harlesden Roxy. He is replaced by Caroline Coon, Simonon's girlfriend. In November Rhodes gets a high court order directing all Clash earnings straight to him.

November 1978
'Give 'Em Enough Rope', the second album, released, followed by the 'Clash Sort It Out Tour' a reference to the problems they have been having with their manager, their music and their record label.

January 1979
The Clash are acclaimed as Best Band in *NME* Readers' Poll, as well as picking up best guitarist (Jones) and single ('White Man in Hammersmith Palais'). In the following month's *Sounds* Readers' Poll they get best band, album and live gig.

February 1979
First brief US tour, with the undiplomatic title 'Pearl Harbour '79'; the opening song for each show is 'I'm So Bored With The U.S.A.' The band fall out with their US record label Epic, but audience reaction is excellent.

June 1979
Caroline Coon's tenure as manager of The Clash comes to an end.

August 1979
'London Calling' recording sessions with maverick producer Guy Stevens.

September-October 1979
Major US tour – the 'Clash Take The Fifth' Tour with support act the Undertones.
Keyboard player Mickey Gallagher, from Ian Dury and the Blockheads, augments
the band; ex-Pink Floyd management company Blackhill, who are involved with
Stiff Records and the Blockheads, take on management responsibilities.

December 1979
The Clash win their battle with CBS to release 'London Calling' at a reduced price,
by taking lower royalties. Album debuts in UK charts at Number 9.

March 1980
Release of the film *Rude Boy*, based around
fictional Clash roadie, but includes live
footage shot over previous 18 months
including the Anti-Nazi League Rally of April
1978. The Clash try and stop the film's
release, as they feel they have moved on.

May 1980
On tour in Europe, where a punk revival is under way, Strummer is arrested in
Hamburg after hitting a particularly violent audience member with his guitar,
though freed when a breathalyser test is negative. Start of a period of problems:
reported unhappiness within the band, who are getting involved with outside
projects: Mick Jones producing his then girlfriend Ellen Foley's album, Strummer
producing London R&B band The Little Roosters, Simonon with a part in a film
called *All Washed Up*.

December 1980
'Sandinista!' is released as a triple album at a single album price, the band
reportedly taking no royalties on the first 200,000 copies to get CBS to put it out
cheaper. It reaches 19 in the UK charts, and later 24 in the US, but is generally
panned by the critics.

January 1981
Strummer and Bernie Rhodes meet by chance. Within a few
weeks Rhodes returns to manage the band.

June 1981
An eight-day residency at Times Square's Bonds International
Casino runs into trouble. Fire brigade restrictions halve the
available capacity. The club is closed indefinitely and $250
million dollars of ticket money are left up in the air until a go-ahead is given with
increased security and fire restrictions. Result: the band are the talk of New York.

Summer 1981
Gigging in the States, The Clash are not around for the riots in UK cities – leads to
predictable comments about their genuine political commitment.

April 1982
Joe Strummer disappears just before beginning of their planned UK 'Know Your
Rights' tour, causing the dates to be postponed. Theories proliferate as to his
departure – a nervous breakdown, a publicity stunt . . . .

May 1982
Strummer is tracked down in Paris, and returns in time to perform at the Lochem
Festival, but almost immediately Topper Headon quits the band, to be replaced
temporarily by original drummer Terry Chimes for a US tour that starts at the end
of the month. 'Combat Rock', produced by Glyn Johns, is released and gets to
Number 2 in the UK charts.

September 1982
At the end of more US dates, The Clash support The Who on their farewell US
tour. *NME* and others ask what has happened to The Clash's philosophy of 'No
Elvis, Beatles or the Rolling Stones'.

May 1983
Pete Howard takes over the drum slot, after 300 applicants have auditioned.

September 1983
Mick Jones is sacked. The official statement says that 'it is felt that Jones had
drifted away from the original idea of The Clash'.

January 1984
New line-up is announced with guitarists Vince White and Nick Sheppard joining Strummer, Simonon and Howard.

May 1985
The Clash go busking round North of England, playing small clubs, pubs, and fans queuing for gigs by the Alarm. Joe Strummer says, if the music press want to know why, 'just tell 'em we've gone absolutely raving mad'.

November 1985
The Clash's final album 'Cut The Crap', released – it reaches UK Number 16, with songs credited to Strummer-Rhodes.
The Clash disbands.

April 1988
Compilation 'The Story Of The Clash, Volume 1' released.

October 1989
Rolling Stone critics make 'London Calling' their top album of Eighties (it had been released in January 1980 in the US).

January 1990
Rumours about Mick Jones's Big Audio Dynamite splitting lead in turn to rumours of The Clash re-forming.

March 1991
The Clash go to Number 1 in the UK singles charts with 'Should I Stay Or Should I Go', re-released after it is used in a Levi's commercial. The band's first Top 10 hit, let alone Number 1.

September 1991
There is press speculation that The Clash have been offered £10 million to reform for a one-off US tour. Similar rumours surface in 1993 and 1995.

THE CAST

Terry Chimes. Born 25 January 1955, Mile End, London. Although he fails an audition as drummer for Jones's London SS (whose New York Dolls influence may have jarred with Chimes's own taste for Led Zep and Free), he is recalled to try out for The Clash in May 1976. Plays with them until November 1976 when the band suggest he leaves because he doesn't care for the violence at some gigs – though more likely that he simply doesn't fit in. Asked to return and help out on the recording of 'White Riot' he supplies drums for the first album. Goes on to form own band Jem, plays with Keith Levene in Cowboys International, and with Generation X. When Topper Headon leaves The Clash in 1982, Chimes agrees to re-join and plays on live dates, but always on a temporary basis. From 1983, Chimes works with Billy Idol and Hanoi Rocks; eventually studies to practise as a chiropractor and acupuncturist.

Caroline Coon. The founder of Release, the drugs/legal aid organisation, Coon is a contributor to *IT*, the late Sixties radical underground paper, before joining *Melody Maker* as regular singles reviewer. An early supporter of punk, Coon runs the first full length interview with The Clash in *Melody Maker*, by which time she is also personally involved with Paul Simonon. When Bernie Rhodes is sacked in October 1978, she takes on the management of The Clash but after six months or so, that semi-official role, and her relationship with Simonon, is over. A collection of her punk writings is published as *1988: The New Wave Punk Rock Explosion*.

Topper Headon. Born Nicholas Headon, 30 May 1955, Bromley, Kent. An accomplished drummer after playing with local Kent bands as a teenager, he tours American military bases with band called the GIs, then on pub rock circuit. After brief time with Mick Jones's London SS, he meets Jones again in March 1977 when The Clash are looking to replace Terry Chimes. Joins officially in April 1977. After five years with the band, during which time he is invited to perform with the New Symphony Orchestra at the Royal Albert Hall in 1981, he is sacked in May 1982 – the most likely reason a heavy drug dependency. Flirts with a number of bands, including a possible collaboration with Mick Jones at the end of 1983.

Finally releases solo album 'Waking Up' in 1986, but is jailed in 1987 for 15 months on charges of supplying heroin. After release rumoured to have become a mini-cab driver. Benefits as lyricist on 'Should I Stay Or Should I Go' from the single's successful 1991 re-release.

Glyn Johns. The producer brought in to create 'Combat Rock' out of the work in progress called 'Rat Patrol From Fort Bragg' has a fine track record with the likes of the Rolling Stones, the Beatles, the Faces and the Who (he is responsible for producing 'Who's Next').

Mick Jones. Born 26 June 1955, South London. In his early years, a fan of the Animals and the Kinks, Jones becomes a huge Mott The Hoople fan during his time at grammar school in Brixton. Starts playing with Hoople-influenced band The Delinquents in 1974, before forming the London SS with Tony James the following year. The London SS, a New York Dolls-style outfit, never plays any gigs, but Jones does get to audition/rehearse with many musicians including Rat Scabies, Topper Headon and Paul Simonon. At this time he meets Bernie Rhodes who becomes involved with the band, and his evolution into The Clash. During his time with The Clash, Jones produces sometime girlfriend Ellen Foley's 1980 album 'Spirit Of St Louis' and co-produces Ian Hunter's 'Short Back'n'Sides' in 1981. Is sacked by Strummer and Simonon in September 1983. After the split with The Clash he forms Big Audio Dynamite, with Don Letts (vocals), Dan Donovan – son of Terence and husband of Patsy Kensit (keyboards), Leo Williams (bass), Greg Roberts (drums). Debut album 'This Is Big Audio Dynamite' is released in 1985, and single 'E=MC^2' just misses UK Top Ten. On second album 'No. 10 Upping Street' (their best placed album) Strummer co-writes and co-produces. Other albums include 'Tighten Up, Vol. 88' (1988) and 'Megatop Phoenix' (1989). Jones guests on Aztec Camera's 'Good Morning Britain' in 1991. Big Audio Dynamite II is formed in 1990 (their highest placed album in the UK is 'Kool-Aid' in 1990, while 'The Globe' makes Number 1 in US college radio alternative charts).

MoDERN iCoNS ●– THE CLASH

Keith Levene. An East Londoner, he meets Mick Jones through a mutual friend and plays in the London SS, and the early Clash line-up, taking lead guitar role. Leaves after a handful of gigs – his last performance with The Clash at the Roundhouse in September 1976. His enduring memorial a co-writing credit for 'What's My Name' on the debut album. After a stint with the Flowers of Romance, which includes Sid Vicious, Palm Olive and Viv Albertine (both later of the Slits) and Rat Scabies, and then in Cowboys International, he links up with and joins John Lydon's Public Image Limited in April 1978.

Other Clash members. Between Terry Chimes and Topper Headon, **Rob Harper** is the drummer on the 1976 'Anarchy' tour. A 27-year-old Sussex University graduate, he has a dozen years' experience on guitar, bass and drums, and has played in a band with Mark Knopfler. After his time with The Clash, Harper plays for the UK Subs, and in the early days of the band that became Adam and the Ants. Following Topper Headon's departure and Terry Chimes's second stint with the band, **Pete Howard** is recruited to The Clash in 1983 via a *Melody Maker* small ad. He has previously played with Bath band Cold Fish. When Mick Jones is fired, two guitarists make it through the *Melody Maker* ad and audition route: **Nick Sheppard**, who had been in Bristol punk act the Cortinas, and Southampton-born student **Vince White**. After The Clash Sheppard is briefly in a band called Head – little known of the others' further careers.

Sandy Pearlman. The producer of 'Give 'Em Enough Rope' is best known for his work with American heavy metal outfit Blue Oyster Cult. Probably selected by The Clash to create a sound more suited to American radio. A stern taskmaster: the album is not complete by the time The Clash have to fulfil tour commitments, and Pearlman insists on subsequent vocal and guitar overdubs in San Francisco, followed by further mixes in NYC – not the punk ethos of raw immediacy. His production work is criticised by UK music writers as 'bombastic' and dubbed 'AOR HM' (Adult-Oriented Rock/Heavy Metal).

Bernie Rhodes. Born in London, Rhodes is active on the fringes of the late Sixties underground and music scene (with Bolan and T. Rex), before going into the motor trade. Starts working with Malcolm McLaren in latter's shops Let It Rock and Sex, through which he is involved in the early days of the Sex Pistols – possibly being the man who found Johnny Rotten. After McLaren takes total control of the Pistols, Rhodes seeks another vehicle – initially the London SS, and then The Clash. As manager, he secures their £100,000 recording deal with a last-minute switch to CBS. By October 1978 tensions, particularly between Rhodes and Mick Jones, have reached the point where Rhodes is sacked. Goes off to set up own club and help steer the early careers of the Specials and Dexys Midnight Runners. In 1981, as The Clash have lost some of their direction, Rhodes returns as manager, at Joe Strummer's suggestion, and oversees the final years, to the extent of taking the production chair on 'Cut The Crap'. Post-Clash, continues in the music business, setting up his own short-lived label, Sacred.

Paul Simonon. Born 15 December 1955, Thornton Heath. Family moves to Ramsgate, where Paul picks up interest in painting from his father, an ex-army insurance agent. Moves to Notting Hill in his early teens with his father, gets place at the Byam Shaw School of Art in October 1974. A chance meeting with Mick Jones towards the end of 1975 leads to an unsuccessful audition as vocalist for the London SS, but Bernie Rhodes and Jones remember Simonon's good looks and suggest he learns bass to join The Clash. A join-the-dots crash course in bass playing follows. Other than a mural in The Clash's rehearsal room, Simonon drops his art until after the band finally splits, then spends a couple of years painting in London and New York (he supplies the front cover of 'Tighten Up, Vol. 88' for Mick Jones's Big Audio Dynamite). Having formed band Havana 3am in late Eighties with Nigel Dixon and Gary Myrick, the group releases eponymous album in 1990.

Guy Stevens. Island's first house producer, Stevens, an ex Mod DJ, plays major role in breaking Spooky Tooth, Free and, above all, Mott The Hoople. Although he has encountered Mick Jones early in Jones's musical career, it is Bernie Rhodes who suggests that Stevens produce The Clash's first demos in 1976. He lives up to his erratic reputation, but is brought back to produce 'London Calling', since CBS/Epic are pressing the band to use a name producer. The sessions in August and September 1979 acquire semi-legendary status, with Stevens attending irregularly, drinking heavily, blowing up the studio television etc. After further problems with alcohol, Stevens dies of a drug overdose in 1981. The band write a tribute to him – 'Midnight To Stevens' – which is included in the 1991 retrospective 'Clash On Broadway'.

 **Joe Strummer.** Born John Mellor, 21 August 1952 in Ankara, Turkey. His father is with the Foreign Office, moving to Cairo, Mexico City and Bonn before settling the family near Croydon, South London. Like many children of families in the diplomatic service, Strummer is sent to a boarding school in Epsom, before getting a place at Central School of Art in 1970. While there he styles himself Woody, after folk-singer Woody Guthrie. Starts getting involved in music, particularly with Newport-based band The Vultures, before forming the 101'ers back in London and giving himself the self-deprecating name Joe Strummer. The 101'ers (called after the house number where he was living and the band started rehearsing) makes their debut in Brixton in September 1974, making a mark on the pub rock circuit, releasing one single 'Keys To Your Heart'. When the band is supported one night by the Sex Pistols, Strummer is knocked out by their performance . . . . Spotted by Jones and Simonon, he joins The Clash in April 1976. After The Clash split he acts in the Alex Cox films *Straight To Hell* (1986) and *Walker* (1987), for which he also writes the soundtrack. He provides some co-production and writing work to BAD's second album, plays with the Pogues on tour in 1988 and 1991, guests on Bob Dylan's 'Down In The Groove' (1988), and forms own band Latino Rockabilly War (psychobilly meets latin and jazz) which releases debut album 'Earthquake Weather' in 1989.

THE BOOKS

Last Gang In Town: The Story And Myth Of The Clash
– Marcus Gray (Fourth Estate) 1995

The Clash: Before And After
– Pennie Smith (Eel Pie) 1980, updated (Plexus) 1991

The Clash: The New Visual Documentary
– Miles, John Tobler & Mal Peachey (Omnibus) 1983, updated 1992

PICTURE CREDITS

Pages 2-3 Julian Yewdall/London Features International (LFI). **Page 5** LFI. **Page 8** Erica Echenberg/Redferns. **Page 11** Ebet Roberts/Redferns. **Page 12** Steve Morley/Redferns. **Page 13** Elaine Bryant/LFI. **Page 14** Ian Dickson/Redferns. **Page 15** Ian Dickson/Redferns. **Page 16** LFI. **Page 17** Adrian Boot/LFI. **Page 18** Ian Dickson/Redferns. **Page 19** Keith Bernstein/Redferns. **Page 20** Ebet Roberts/Redferns. **Page 21** Adrian Boot/LFI. **Page 22** Fraser Gray/Redferns. **Page 24** (t) Steve Morley/Redferns; (b) Adrian Boot/LFI. **Pages 26-7** Ian Dickson/Redferns. **Page 29** (t) Ebet Roberts/Redferns; (b) Courtesy of CBS Records. **Pages 30-1** (t) LFI; (b) Erica Echenberg/Redferns. **Page 33** (t) Fraser Gray/Redferns; (m) Adrian Boot/LFI; (b) Elaine Bryant/LFI. **Page 34** (l) Val Wilner/Redferns; (r) LFI. **Pages 36-7** Keith Bernstein/Redferns. **Page 37** Ebet Roberts/Redferns. **Page 38** Keith Bernstein/Redferns. **Page 39** Ian Dickson/Redferns. **Page 41** (t) Caroline Coon/LFI; (b) Keith Bernstein/Redferns. **Pages 42-3** Ian Dickson/Redferns. **Page 45** Fraser Grey/Redferns. **Page 46** LFI. **Page 47** Ebet Roberts/Redferns. **Page 49** (t) Keith Bernstein/Redferns; (b) Erica Echenberg/Redferns. **Page 50** (l) Erica Echenberg/Redferns; (r) Steve Morley/Redferns. **Pages 52-3** Ebet Roberts/Redferns. **Page 55** Keith Bernstein/Redferns. **Page 57** (l) Redferns; (r) Ebet Roberts/Redferns. **Page 58** Ebet Roberts/Redferns. **Page 61** (t) LFI; (b) Erica Echenberg/Redferns. **Pages 62-3** Summa/LFI. **Page 63** Michel Linssen/Redferns. **Page 65** (t) SKR Photos/LFI; (b) Keith Bernstein/Redferns. **Page 66** Erica Echenberg/Redferns. **Page 67** Courtesy of CBS Records. **Pages 68-9** Ebet Roberts/Redferns. **Page 69** Courtesy of CBS Records. **Page 70** Courtesy of CBS Records. **Pages 70-1** (t) Ebet Roberts/Redferns; (b) Keith Bernstein/Redferns. **Page 73** (l) Ebet Roberts/Redferns; (r) LFI. **Pages 74-5** Ebet Roberts/Redferns. **Page 75** Kevin Cummins/LFI. **Page 76** Kevin Cummins/LFI. **Page 77** (l) Kevin Cummins/LFI; (r) Ebet Roberts/Redferns. **Page 78** Summa/LFI. **Page 79** Keith Bernstein/Redferns. **Page 80** Fraser Gray/Redferns. **Page 81** Ebet Roberts/Redferns. **Page 82** Ian Dickson/Redferns. **Page 83** Elaine Bryant/LFI. **Page 84** Ebet Roberts/Redferns. **Page 85** Ebet Roberts/Redferns. **Page 86** LFI. **Page 87** Val Wilmer/Redferns. **Page 89** Ebet Roberts/Redferns. **Page 90** Ian Dickson/Redferns. **Page 91** Keith Bernstein/Redferns. **Page 92** Julian Yewdall/LFI. **Page 93** Ebet Roberts/Redferns.

Every effort has been made to contact copyright holders.
If any ommissions do occur the publisher would be
delighted to give full credit in subsequent reprints and editions.